INFLATION

A Money Power Book

by David A. Adler

Illustrated by Tom Huffman

INFLATION

When Prices Go Up, Up, Up

A GROLIER COMPANY

Franklin Watts

New York   London   Sydney   Toronto

1985

To my brother Joe

R.L. 3.0 Spache Revised Formula

Library of Congress Cataloging in Publication Data

Adler, David A.
  Inflation: when prices go up, up, up.

  (A Money power book)
  Summary: Discusses the reasons for inflation, the
effects it has on the spending power of the government
and the individual, the influence of supply and demand,
and what can be done to curb this phenomena.
  1. Inflation (Finance)—Juvenile literature. [1. Inflation
(Finance)] I. Huffman, Tom, ill. II. Title. III. Series.
HG221.5.A345   1985   332.4'1   85-8989
ISBN 0-531-04899-3

Prices keep changing.

In 1945, at the Coney Island amusement park, cotton candy cost ten cents. A ride on the carousel was fourteen cents.

5

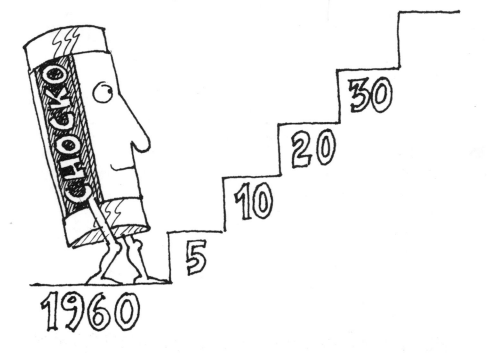

In 1960 a chocolate bar cost five cents. A daily newspaper cost five cents, too. And a loaf of bread cost twenty cents.

Cotton candy, carousel rides, chocolate, newspapers, and bread cost much more today. Prices have gone up.

Even in the past few years, prices for bread, milk, shoes, books, and other things have gone up. When prices are going up, we have inflation.

Inflation doesn't mean that prices are high. It means that prices are changing. They're going up. Of course, not all prices would be changing at the same rate.

7

In a time of inflation some prices might be going up quickly. Others might be going up slowly. Some prices might not be changing at all. Some might even be going down. But during a period of inflation most prices are rising. The average family spends more and more each week.

Inflation means prices are going up. Once we have inflation, it is important to know how fast prices are going up.

Some inflations are mild, with prices going up only 2 to 3 percent a year. This means that if families spend an average of $100 each week, by the end of the year they'll be spending about $102 a week.

But then there is inflation that is not so mild. Prices rise faster. With an inflation rate of 10 percent, prices would more than double every seven and a half years.

With an inflation rate of 10 percent, a toy or game that cost eight dollars today would cost more than sixteen dollars in seven and a half years. Of course, for that to happen, the inflation rate of 10 percent would have to continue for those seven and a half years.

Inflation is a problem for people with savings. The money they have is losing its value. It buys less.

People often talk of the "shrinking dollar." A dollar gets its value from what it can buy. During a period of inflation, each dollar buys less than it did before. Its value is shrinking.

In 1940 a loaf of white bread cost eight cents. Each dollar bought twelve and a half loaves of bread.

1960$ 1980'S$

Twenty years later, in 1960, a loaf of white bread cost twenty cents. Then a dollar bought only five loaves.

By the early 1980s one dollar bought less than two loaves of bread.

Since 1940 the dollar has steadily lost value.

Inflation is a real problem for most people. Many working people are paid salaries, a certain amount each week or month. The salaries they're paid often do not rise quickly enough to keep up with inflation.

Many older people have fixed incomes. Each month they get a certain amount of money from a pension or retirement fund. The amount of money they get doesn't change. But during inflation prices do change. As prices go up, the monthly income of older people buys less and less. And the value of the money they have saved goes down, too.

How do we know how quickly prices are rising? How do we know the rate of inflation?

The government keeps checking the prices of food, clothing, medicines, and other items. They check the prices of about four hundred items every month in many different cities all across the United States. The costs of these items form the **Consumer Price Index.** A rise in the Consumer Price Index is a good measure of the rate of inflation.

But why do prices go up?

Sometimes costs push prices up. When the cost of steel, glass, and other materials that are used to make cars goes up, the cost of a new car will go up too. The wages paid to automobile workers can also push prices up. If their wages go up, the price of a new car will go up too. When costs push prices up, we have **cost-push** inflation.

There are times when people have the money to buy more toys, clothes, food, and cars. If not enough is being produced, the prices of the items that are available go up. This is called **demand-pull** inflation. The demand for more goods pulls prices up.

Often, after a war, there is a demand-pull inflation. During wartime a great many people work to build the machinery of war—guns, tanks, bullets, and bombs. But the things they want to buy with the money they have earned are not available. The country's factories are busy making guns and tanks, not toys and shoes.

After the war, workers want to spend the money they have saved. They want to spend their money on things they could not buy in wartime—toys, shoes, clothes, cars, and houses. Soldiers returning home want to spend the money they have saved. But often there are just not enough peacetime goods available. The demand for peacetime goods *pulls* prices up.

The cause of most inflation is a combination of cost-push and demand-pull. Costs are pushing prices up. The demand for more goods is pulling prices up. This is called a push-pull inflation.

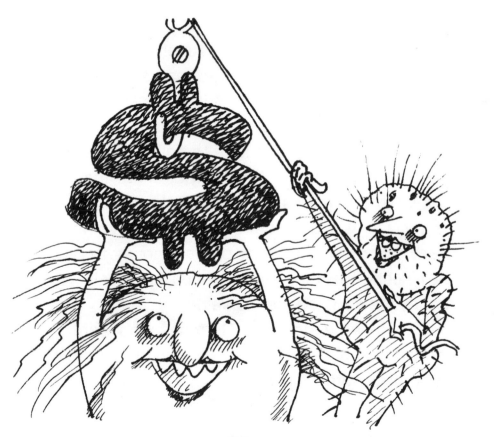

In every inflation, prices go up. But in some countries prices might go up slowly. They have a mild inflation. At the same time, in other countries, prices might go up quickly. Prices go up quickly in a wild, or runaway, inflation.

In Germany after the first World War, prices went wild. Before the war, in 1914, just about four German marks could buy one American dollar. By early 1922 almost two hundred marks were needed to exchange for one dollar. But that was only the beginning. Several months later it took more than one thousand German marks to equal the value of a dollar. By the end of 1923 it took more than forty *billion* German marks to exchange for just one U.S. penny. The war had cost the German government a great deal of money. They printed money to pay their debts. But they printed much too much. The money they printed lost its value.

There were stories of Germans who went shopping with wheelbarrows filled with money and came back with only a small bag of groceries.

The inflation in Hungary during and just after the second World War was even worse. Items that cost just a few Hungarian pengös before the war cost *trillions* and *trillions* of pengös after the war. At one point it was estimated that prices in Hungary were doubling every three to four hours. An item costing just five pengös one morning would cost more than four hundred pengös the next day.

A wild runaway inflation, like the inflations in Germany and Hungary, is called **hyper-inflation.**

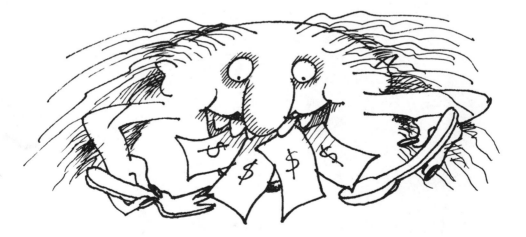

What happens during hyper-inflation?

As prices go up, up, up, the country's money becomes worth less and less. The money people have saved becomes almost worthless.

What do people do during a period of hyper-inflation? Well, they certainly don't want to hold onto their money. The longer they keep it, the less it's worth.

During the German hyper-inflation, workers were paid more than once a day. And as soon as they were paid, they ran out to spend the money.

Of course, this constant spending only made the inflation worse. The demand for things pulled prices up. No one wanted to hold onto marks. Marks had lost their value. People wanted to own things like food, clothing, and furniture. People were willing to pay almost any price for things rather than hold onto German marks.

After a while, in both Germany and Hungary, people wanted to be paid with things and not money. They began trading firewood for bread or milk. When people are paid with things and not money, it is a **barter** system.

What do people do to fight the effects of high rates of inflation?

Workers' unions try to get automatic **cost-of-living** adjustments. If prices go up, so does their pay.

People with savings try not to hold onto dollars. Dollars lose value in an inflation. People buy gold, land, valuable art, stocks, and other investments. During an inflation they expect these investments to go up in price, "to keep up with inflation."

How do governments fight inflation?

In wartime they might pass laws keeping prices and wages at certain levels. They might **ration** important items. Each family would be allowed to buy only a certain amount of gasoline, milk, and meat each month.

A government can also raise taxes. If people pay higher taxes, they have less money to spend. With less money, there's less demand to pull prices up.

Governments spend huge amounts of money each year for schools, roads, tanks, and guns. In inflation, governments might cut their own spending. By spending less of their own money, the people who work for the government will have less money to spend. And with less money to spend, there's less demand to pull prices up.

Inflation means more than just prices going up. It means that money is losing its value. It means that a young family might not be able to afford the price of a new home. It means that old people might not be able to buy all that they need. Inflation is a real problem for people and their governments.